# PERTH
## 150 YEARS

## CITY OF PERTH
## 1829-1979

# PERTH
## 150 YEARS

PHOTOGRAPHY BY
MICHAEL MORCOMBE,
RICHARD WOLDENDORP AND OSKAR OPITZ.

TEXT BY MARGARET MACOBOY

EDITED BY DON HUNT

The graceful black swan, a proud symbol
for the City of Perth emblem, the Western
Australian flag and, most recently,
the State's 150th birthday celebrations.

# PERTH
## 150 YEARS

## CONTENTS

International Standard Book Number 0-9595533-0-4
Copyright © 1979 by publisher
• Jackson Hunt & Company Pty. Limited
Corner Outram & Hay Streets, West Perth, Western Australia.
Typesetter • Insight Photosetting Services
Scanned Colour Separations • J. Gibbney & Sons Pty. Ltd.
Printer • Muhlings Pty. Ltd.
Binder • Printers Trade Services
Editor • D. de V. Hunt
Printed in Western Australia.

"Siska," the largest aluminium sloop ever built in Australia, is pictured on trials in the Swan River, before participating in the Parmelia Race, Plymouth to Perth. This was one of the major events of Western Australia's 150th year.

Even today, kangaroos are found in bushland
surrounding Perth.

On pages 4 and 5 following: The extraordinary
Pinnacles, an ancient petrified forest within
a few hours' drive of Perth.

In the Kimberley region in the far north of
the State, this Frilled Lizard strikes
a spectacular pose of bluff ferocity.

Left: An eternal battle rages between sea and rock at the Fitzgerald River National Park, on the rugged Southern Ocean coast.

In the North-West of the State, the sun rises on the Kennedy Ranges.

Dawn softens the jagged outline of the
Kimberley coastline, near Yampi Sound.

Giant sand dunes invade the land near
Northcliffe on the southern coast.

Right: Towering cliffs at Geikie Gorge in the Kimberley bear witness to the passing of millions of years.

White sand beaches stretch beyond the horizon at Lancelin, a fishing and holiday centre north of Perth.

Left: Paperbark trees cast shadowy patterns over the surface of Lake Jandakot, near Perth.

The icy beauty of a jewel cave near Yallingup in the South West.

"The fishing's great" at Kalbarri, a popular
holiday spot, a day's drive north of Perth.


Right:  Lush pasture land in Western
Australia's abundant South West corner.

Harvesting the golden wheat, a traditional source of Western Australia's riches.

On pages 20 and 21 following: This early morning grazing scene is typical of much of Western Australia where sheep outnumber people more than 25 times.

On page 22 following: The "Muzzleloaders" guards of the Reformed 63rd Regiment of Foot, re-enact the colonial past at the Barracks Archway, Perth.

The velvety kangaroo paw, the State's distinctive wildflower emblem.

Right: The Perth region abounds in bird and plant species. Here, a New Holland Honeyeater probes a banksia in search of nectar.

# PERTH'S FIRST 150 YEARS

## PARMELIA PIONEERS

The passing of 150 years is just the briefest flash in the history of Rome, Jerusalem or Peking.

In Australia, however, it spans the entire life of Perth, the largest city on the Western seaboard.

When the first British settlers disembarked from the transport "Parmelia" and erected their humble camp on the banks of the broad Swan River in 1829, they opened the first chapter in the story of a city.

It is a story with all the elements of a rattling good yarn. The struggle, poverty and perseverance of those early years eventually earned their reward in the great gold boom of the 1890's. Perth leapt overnight into an age of prosperity and rapid growth which transformed it into the bustling, beautiful city it is today.

Those first pioneers must have sensed the significance of their endeavour, for they staged the foundation ceremony with all the aplomb a tiny band of settlers could muster.

On August 12, 1829, in honour of the birthday of His Majesty, King George IV, a naval officer's wife felled a tree 19 km upriver at the foot of a long, wooded bluff which, as Mount Eliza, still dominates the skyline of Perth. As a contemporary account observed, the party then "fired volleys, made speeches and gave several cheers" to celebrate the birth of a new British settlement so far from home.

The choice of the name Perth, however, rankled at least one proud Englishman, who grumbled at the "imprudence in calling the Capital of Swan River by the insignificant name of Perth." He concluded the colony was a place where only the "Scotch interest" would prevail. In the first few years at least he was right for the dominant figure of the early colony was the Governor, a Scottish naval captain, James Stirling. He had previously visited the region on a voyage of exploration in March, 1827 and had been greatly impressed.

Stirling's vision of a "rich and romantic land" watered by the broad reaches of the Swan River fired such interest in England that the newspapers coined it "Swan River Mania."

The prospect of voyaging to the other side of the world appealed to all classes...artisans, labourers, substantial merchants, retired officers, Waterloo veterans and even gentry, all seeking a new and prosperous way of life. The "Parmelia" pioneers included surgeons, surveyors, master mariners, a boat-builder and an agriculturist. The only notable omissions were convicts, for the colony was to be entirely for free settlers.

More pioneers quickly followed the first boatloads and by Christmas 1830, the Swan River Colony boasted a population of 1500.

## A HARSH BEGINNING

Sadly, few had any idea of the hardships and struggle which faced them. A harsh, unfamiliar climate of summer heat and heavy winter rains made adjustment to their new surroundings very difficult.

Roads were either dust bowls in summer or impassable quagmires after winter rains. The early settlers' problems were compounded by heavy timber and undergrowth which made clearing difficult. A hasty and ill-planned land distribution system led to grumbling and disillusion. The settlers also had to contend with Aborigines determined to protect their traditional hunting grounds. Hostility finally flared into the Battle of Pinjarra in 1834, when one white and 15 to 20 Aborigines died.

Most of all, the colony's intense isolation proved an immense hurdle. 14,500 km of ocean separated the tiny settlement from London and even Adelaide, Perth's nearest neighbour after 1837, was more than 2,700 km distant. The Indian Ocean and Nullarbor Plain acted as formidable barriers which discouraged both investment and new, urgently needed settlers.

By 1850, twenty one years after foundation, the population of the whole colony numbered only 5,900. Most were clustered around the Swan River, the colony's lifeblood and only highway. The Perth district had less than 3,000 residents when, in September 1856, Queen Victoria declared the township should be a Bishop's See, which conferred the title of city on the Swan River Colony. Settlement stretched downriver toward the colony's port of Fremantle and upriver into the fertile Swan Valley, where farmers began experimenting with stock and crops.

*The founding of Perth on the banks of the Swan River on August 12, 1829, is depicted in this scene by G. Pitt Morison.*

## THE SOCIAL NICETIES

However, the first citizens of Perth were, in the main, a hardy breed determined to fashion a new life despite the hardships. And that meant preserving at least some of the traditions of the old life. The class distinctions of Britain lingered on with elegant soirées for the gentry, while the "more common sort of settler" amused himself on the river or in the numerous taverns which soon sprang up.

A constant round of dinner parties encouraged a taste for roast swan, parrot pie and kangaroo, which reminded diners of English hare. Musical evenings, riding parties, hunting, picnics, regattas and a regular succession of balls enlivened the social life of the gentry. An early Governor's Ball encouraged a new arrival to record in his diary, "I had no idea there would be so much society here so much gaiety, so much dressing." In fact, social life was essential as a morale-booster for the gentry.

Life did not smile so kindly on many of the poorer settlers who battled primitive working and living conditions and occasionally, destitution, to make their way in the new colony. The tradition of part-payment of wages in rum contributed to drunkenness, an early problem fostered by loneliness and despair.

## THE RELUCTANT RESCUERS

The Swan River Colony languished till, in June 1850, it embarked on a dramatic new phase. The first shipload of convicts arrived in response to the colonists' urgings for more labour and capital. They decided the only way to achieve both, was to abandon their ideal of a free colony on which "no taint of convictism shall ever fall."

Eighteen years of convict labour greatly changed the face of Perth. Substantial public and private buildings, essential public works including a new causeway linking the main settlement to the southern bank of the river and durable, all-weather roads were constructed.

Roads were a constant problem because of unsuitable materials. With convict labour, however, a new method of cutting stout sections of jarrah hardwood as foundations was conceived. The sections, dubbed, "Governor Hampton's Cheeses" after an able but autocratic governor of the time, were highly durable. Nevertheless, clouds of dust from the sandy verges still lingered as a discomfort.

The more thoughtful of the convicts must have felt the bitter irony of two of their first building tasks... gaols at Fremantle and Perth. The Fremantle Gaol, completed in 1859, still houses prisoners, but the Old Perth Gaol, completed three years earlier, has been transformed into a charming museum of colonial history. Picnic tables set up in sunny courtyards can't quite dispel the sense of misery which still lingers, more than a century later, in the cold stone cell blocks.

Other early convict constructions included a hospital and an imposing limestone building at Fremantle distinguished by Dutch gables and Gothic cloisters. It was originally built to house the colony's criminally insane, but today it gives little hint of its grim past. Instead, it contains a superb collection of the State's maritime history, an art gallery and craft workshops. The building at last seems to have found the role suited to its graceful lines.

Many of Perth's most impressive buildings including the Town Hall, the Cloisters, Government House, the Pensioners Barracks, and the charming gabled Deanery date from this period. The once proud Barracks has suffered most with the passing years. All that remains is its battlemented Tudor gateway standing at the western end of St. George's Terrace, the boulevard which is the city's commercial centre.

It was also the heyday of elegant townhouses, mainly concentrated at the eastern end of St. George's Terrace overlooking the expanse of Perth Water.

Public buildings of the era are instantly recognisable today by their distinctive red and cream chequered brickwork laid in a pattern known as Flemish Bond. Clay for the bricks was dug from small pits which were later transformed into picturesque lakes and blended into the landscaping of Queen's Gardens.

The end of the convict era in 1869 meant an end to the steady stream of British Government money needed to administer the system. Perth, though now assured of survival, marked time as the younger cities of Melbourne, Adelaide and Brisbane flourished. Isolation, and the hardships and risks it entailed, threatened to make Perth the Cinderella capital of Australia.

## GOLDEN DECADE

This lonely existence was suddenly shattered by the magic word 'gold.' A rapid succession of finds, climaxing in the rich discoveries at Coolgardie and Kalgoorlie in 1892/3, brought a stream of hopeful fortune-hunters to the colony. Prospectors struck it rich in the arid goldfields and retired to the comfort of the city to build splendid homes. Impressive public buildings including government offices, a library and a museum, as well as hotels, theatres, and shops sprang up as the city flourished.

The Perth Mint still one of only two in Australia, remains today as a reminder of the importance attached to the gold discoveries.

Expanding trade, railway and telegraph construction and the granting of responsible self-government in 1890 marked the beginning of a sparkling new phase in the history of Perth. The gold rush had established Perth as a true city at last.

As the next few decades revealed, the benefits of the rush long outlived the boom itself.

The immense wealth generated by gold was directed to developing vast wheat growing areas and Perth matured in its role as the business heart of Western Australia.

Edwardian Perth was a city of flamboyant prosperity with De Dions and Fords jostling for space on the city streets among horse-drawn cabs. New wealth found expression in fine suburban homes, floridly decorated in the style of the times. City streets became cluttered in a welter of telegraph and electricity wires which shouted the new priorities—prosperity before beauty. Many who had come with the gold rushes stayed on to farm, or, like the large Chinese population, to provide essential services such as market gardening.

Gold had attracted people of all nationalities, but the British influence in Perth remained predominant. The city's growing sense of patriotic unity revealed itself in an enthusiastic response to the call for recruits in both the Boer War and Great War. In terms of manpower and financial aid offered, Western Australia led the rest of the Commonwealth.

When peace had settled once more, the world rejoiced in the "golden age" of the 1920's. Its tumultuous effect reverberated as far as Perth where people enjoyed increasing material comfort and such luxuries as telephones and motor cars became more commonplace. As Perth's centenary year approached, its citizens could look back with pride at their achievements.

## CENTENARY CELEBRATIONS

The city's centenary year of 1929 was marked by two events which symbolised the successful struggle to overcome isolation and obscurity.

As an indication of emerging status, Perth was honoured with a lord mayoralty and the 'tyranny of distance' was significantly reduced by the inauguration of the first regular air service between Perth and the Eastern States.

The world depression of the 1930's affected Western Australia later, but just as harshly, as the rest of the country. The old saviour, gold, once again came to the rescue as many of the unemployed were absorbed in the goldmining industry. Wheat farming, however, was severely hit by the slump in world markets and did not recover til World War II.

Sadly, it took this second major world upheaval to firmly unite the West with the rest of Australia. As in the Great War, Western Australia contributed generously to the war effort, and, in doing so, embarked on a programme of industrialization.

In the first few years of post-war prosperity, the State's first major industrial complex was established at Kwinana on Cockburn Sound. Diversification of industry and continued demand for the State's primary produce saw Perth continue on a path of slow, if unspectacular growth.

## A CITY TAKES ITS PLACE IN THE WORLD

But history was poised to repeat itself and launch the city into yet another exciting new era.

Vast mineral wealth, this time iron ore and later nickel, bauxite, ilmenite and natural gas attracted keen investment interest during the 1960's.

Fortunes were made overnight, giant steel and concrete office towers dwarfed the charming colonial buildings in St. George's Terrace and chattering telexes linked Perth to the financial centres of the world.

That decade of hectic development has left an indelible imprint on the city in the shape of multi-storey commercial offices. Residential development is being actively encouraged in the city centre, but most Perth residents prefer to live as they have always done, in their own house on their own block of land. The city's population of over 800,000 has spilled over into long corridors of growth to the north, east and south. Affluent suburbs of attractive brick homes set in cool green lawns continue to develop at a rate faster than any other capital in Australia.

The gracious homes of the early, well-to-do settlers now occupy choice real estate overlooking the Swan River, the water playground of clerks and millionaires alike.

Perth's natural beauty after 150 years of growth is still largely unimpaired by progress. Careful planning has led to an harmonious mingling of industry, commerce and residential needs to create a city of distinctive charm. The vitality of expanding business and fast growth is tempered by the tranquillity of the city's open spaces, the delightful parks, the long sparkling beaches and, above all, the broad, clear waters of the magnificent Swan River.

This impressive limestone building, now a museum, is one of Australia's finest examples of colonial gothic architecture.

Right: The Cloisters, first built as a school in 1858,
is now incorporated into a modern shopping
and office complex.

70,000 people gathered on the banks of the
Swan to usher in Perth's 150th Year in 1979,
with a New Year's Eve fireworks spectacular.

Right: Twentieth century concrete dwarfs
the colonnaded grace of Perth's Treasury
Buildings.

Government House, Perth's vice-regal residence
since 1864, is secluded from the city bustle
among lush gardens.

Left: In recent years, the Perth Town Hall, once the city's outstanding landmark, has surrendered its pre-eminence to the 33 storey, 133m high City Centre.

A study in contrasts: Victorian ornamentation in floodlit harmony with Seventies simplicity.

Right: Perth's port is Fremantle, where the
Victorian charm of the Town Hall harmonises
with casual, sunny plazas.

The ivy covered walls and glorious gardens of
St. George's College suggest a cloistered English
setting at the University of Western Australia.

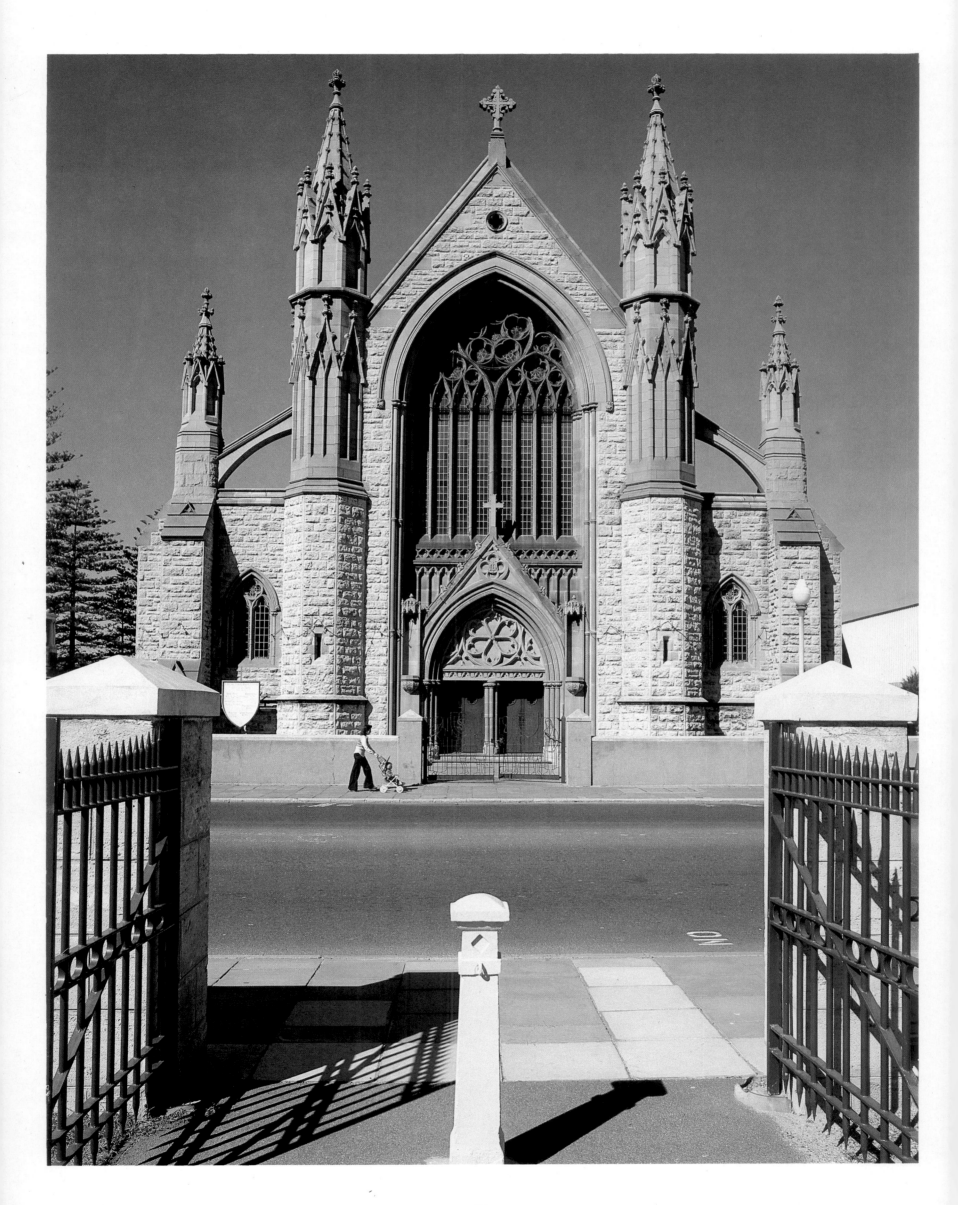

On pages 36 and 37 following: Rural beauty
still lives on at historic Tranby House, Maylands.

Left: The striking neo-Gothic architecture
of Fremantle's St. Patrick's Church.

Morning sun highlights the grace of St. Mary's
Cathedral, situated on a crest overlooking
Perth.

Woodloes Homestead, built in 1874, was one of the
first architect-designed homes in the Swan
River Colony...

. . . and inside, a bedroom has been faithfully restored
to Victorian comfort.

Right: The austere interior of Perth's Old Gaol, now a museum, harks back to the convict era.

Attractive iron lacework at Woodbridge,
a Victorian mansion built on the site of
Governor Stirling's "cottage ornée"
at Guildford.

Right: The Old Mill on the southern bank of
the Swan River at South Perth, once
withstood a siege by natives in search of flour.

The Perth Mint, one of only two in Australia,
recalls the rich gold finds of the "Roaring Nineties."

Perth's early reliance on the sea is displayed
at the Maritime Museum, Fremantle.

On page 46 following: Autumn splendour along Mounts Bay Road, a scenic highway which traces the Swan River to Perth.

The charming Victorian Deanery brings an air of romance to St. George's Terrace.

# PERTH AND ITS PEOPLE

## ALWAYS A SMILE

One word instantly springs to mind in describing Perth and its people.

Friendly.

It is the single characteristic which has been most frequently written about, talked about and fondly remembered by visitors to Perth.

The easy-going cheerful informality is a refreshing 'reviver' for Americans, Europeans or even "Eastern Staters" accustomed to the brisk impersonality of their big cities.

Naturally, size has something to do with it.

Perth's population is big enough to generate a cosmopolitan vitality yet still small enough to preserve an unsophisticated charm.

It is rare to walk through the Hay Street Mall, the heart of the central shopping district, without encountering a cheery grin or at least a welcoming nod. Perth people are happy and it shows.

The tumultuous mineral bonanza of the Sixties dramatically quickened the pace of life, but it left untouched those quiet, understated qualities which have always been Perth's charm.

People are considerate to each other in a way reminiscent of old world courtesy. It is still possible to saunter down a busy street without being elbowed out of the way. People volunteer directions, tell you the time, even chat on buses. It's just part of the spirit of co-operation which makes Perth such an easy place to live.

Perth's friendliness has its roots in the pioneering past. The intense isolation of the new colony bred a close-knit community where everyone needed to support each other on both an emotional and physical level.

The critical shortage of labour forced settlers of all classes to put aside artificial barriers and work side by side.

Without doubt, Perth's wonderful balmy climate which lures everyone outdoors for open-air fun has been another strong unifying influence.

It's so easy to slip into first-name familiarity over an impromptu backyard pool party or a steak grilled to perfection on an outdoor barbecue. Any stiffness or formality melts away in the common enjoyment of simple pleasures.

In recent years, this enviable lifestyle has made Perth a magnet for new settlers and an increasing number of tourists. The latest census confirms Perth as Australia's fastest growing capital city, and likely to be next in size only to Sydney and Melbourne by the end of the century.

Yet, even as new homes spread out in an ever-increasing radius from the hub of the city centre, Perth remains, above all, a 'people city.'

## REWARDING WALKING

Airy plazas and malls, arcades crammed with speciality shops selling goods from every corner of the world and luxuriant garden settings soften the city bustle into a delightful pedestrian environment.

Sweet-scented potted plants and trees in the Hay Street Mall have transformed the central city into a shopper's domain. Comfortable benches shaded by coloured umbrellas are perfect for resting weary feet and 'watching the world go by.' During the annual Festival of Perth, strolling musicians, artisans selling their silver, copper and leather work and zany street theatre make the Mall Perth's most vibrant and colourful thoroughfare.

The restful pedestrian atmosphere continues further north in the central city area in Forrest Place, the scene of spirited political meetings during the highly-charged days of the mid 1970's. Now political oratory has given way to lunch time concerts as entertainment for city workers relaxing in the plaza which has recently been transformed into a mall.

Just a short walk away, the city reveals an entirely different character, the intriguing Tudor charm of London Court. Old gables and diamond-pane windows which could have stepped straight out of

*In Perth there's always time for a laugh, even cooking up a fast-order crepe.*

Shakespeare's London, are a constant source of wonder to visitors. The arcade, built in the 1930's by a flamboyant mining entrepreneur, offers delightful browsing in tiny shops each displaying a gilded name shield.

Multi-level arcades, built in rapid succession during the heady days of the mining boom, offer up-to-the-minute convenience and comfort.

Silent escalators whisk pedestrians to shops, restaurants, taverns and cinemas without the need to step outside into the street. But when they do, the streets, even in the centre of the city, are almost invariably bathed in welcoming sunshine. The pervading gloom of so many cities where towering skyscrapers banish all sunshine never descends on Perth. Giant office towers have been designed with thought for space, light and an unobstructed view of the sky. Many are surrounded by spacious plazas adding a Mediterranean touch of outdoor gaiety.

Tall buildings stretch along major
thoroughfares east and west of the city centre.

## EASY LIVING

Perth is even mercifully free of traffic jams – all the more remarkable considering the ownership ratio of 1.9 persons to every vehicle is one of the world's highest.

A well-planned system of freeways and 'ring' roads allows traffic to bypass the city centre and speed to the suburbs stretching north, south and east. Where a 15 km trip can stretch out to a frustrating 30 or 40 minutes in many cities, it can be a 10 minute 'breeze' in Perth.

The sense that Perth really is the heart of the 'lucky country' is most apparent in the lush green affluence of the suburbs. With very rare exceptions Perth people live well. The sparkling clear water of the Swan River is a superb backdrop to old homes set in sprawling riverside gardens or modern villas just a stone's throw from one of Australia's finest venues for yachting, swimming, prawning and skiing.

For others who centre their lives around the beach, the Indian Ocean coast is an irresistible magnet. Coastal suburbs north and south of the city are architectural showpieces. What was once mile upon mile of sandy coastal plain is now transformed into elegant suburbs where homes are carefully designed to take advantage of their spectacular setting.

The older inner-city suburbs which could most easily decline into neglect, instead sport a distinctive flair. Subiaco, Leederville, Wembley and North Perth have, in the past decade, become the last word in fashion among renovators. Wrought iron lacework and carefully restored interiors preserve the style of generations ago. Browsing for antiques or some charming piece of bric-a-brac is a weekend delight in many small shops and galleries dotted around these older areas.

Fremantle, the colony's oldest settlement, has perhaps more than any other suburb, a distinctive individuality. It stems partly from the port's historic buildings and partly from the people who have chosen to live there.

Portuguese, Spanish and Italian fishermen live in modest stone homes in South Fremantle handy to their livelihood, the sea. In recent years, young professional couples with a flair for renovation have revitalised the port by restoring charming terrace houses to their former style.

Fremantle's original market built in 1897, has been re-opened with careful thought to preserving its 'rough and ready' Victorian flavour. On Fridays and Saturdays it becomes a colourful bustle of spruikers shouting their wares and shoppers hunting among the stalls of Victoriana, handicrafts or home-made jams and pates in search of a bargain or a tempting taste.

Darlington, an outer suburb nestled among the tall gums of the Darling Range, is Perth's artistic colony. Painters, potters and jewellers draw inspiration from the natural bushland which surrounds them. Many other areas, too, have a highly individualistic flavour. Midland has its vignerons, Spearwood its market gardeners, Booragoon its rising young executives, Kalamunda its orchardists and Medina its hard-hat steelworkers who earn their livelihood in the nearby Kwinana industrial complex.

Regardless of different incomes and attitudes, Perth is a strongly unified city. The urge to conform was, until recently, a powerful trait. It even revealed itself in a typical housing style of a single storey bungalow which made the most of Perth's abundant space and sunshine. Now, however, home designs reflect a far greater diversity stemming from international influences. Elegant town houses and home units clustered around a central leafy courtyard suggest a Riviera touch in a distinctly Australian landscape.

Whatever the style – bungalow, two-storey mansion or town house – it's sure to be surrounded by a carefully tended garden. "A man's home is his castle" is the universal attitude and gardens abound in native plants and eucalypts, which are enjoying an upsurge of popularity because of their beauty and hardiness.

The lawns and trees seem all the greener in Perth's crisp, clear air. Visitors are instantly aware of the clarity of the light which highlights colours in brilliant postcard hues.

*Weekend browsing at the Fremantle Markets, an original Victorian marketplace now restored to its former use.*

The grime and grit of other cities is banished from Perth where the girls always seem to have lustrous shining hair and unblemished complexions. Their reputation for loveliness has carried to all corners of the world, helped no doubt, by poster scenes of bikini-clad bodies soaking up the sun on gleaming, white-sand beaches.

Any suggestion of polluted city air is swept away almost every summer afternoon by the revered "Fremantle Doctor," the cooling breeze which flows in from the ocean.

When Captain James Stirling first gazed upon the Swan River Valley and described it as a 'rich and romantic land,' he prophesied accurately for the future.

The city of Perth which grew in this lyrical setting deserves superlatives. It can truly claim to be one of the world's most beautiful cities, one that has gained rather than suffered from growth and prosperity.

On pages 52 and 53 following: Perth people know
how to 'relax in a State of excitement'.
Here, the Swan River is perfect for an
afternoon's fishing.

Right: Modern buildings reach for the sky as if to
symbolise the city's striving towards the future.

You can hear everything from baroque
to rock in the intimate setting of the
Perth Concert Hall.

51

Black swans, ducks and gulls come in their
thousands to be fed at Lake Monger.

Life in Perth has a rare serenity. A family
group relaxes under the spreading branches
of a Moreton Bay fig tree.

Glass fronted glamour in one of Perth's
many modern arcades.

Right: While work goes on in offices above,
a family paddles at the base of Council House,
the administrative centre for the City of Perth.

A lunchtime stroll to restaurants and
boutiques beneath the towering offices of
St. George's Terrace.

Perth's artistic life has a youthful vitality.

On page 64 following: Surf, sand and a bottle of suntan oil...Perth's white sand beaches stretch for 50 kilometres.

Right:   Shakespeare might almost have felt at home in Perth's incongruously Elizabethan London Court.

The thrill of a close finish at picturesque Ascot racecourse.

# PERTH'S WATER PLAYGROUNDS

A love of the water and its endless opportunities for pleasure unites Perth people.

It could hardly be otherwise.

Perth's setting is dominated by water... on one hand, the broad sweep of the Swan River and, on the other, the long, sun-drenched coastline of the Indian Ocean.

A home with sweeping views over yacht-studded bays or crashing ocean breakers is a dream come true for many people. The urge to 'be by the water' has been ingrained into Perth's population since the first settlers disembarked in Cockburn Sound and ventured up the Swan River. As they rowed the 19 kms upstream to found the new city at the foot of Mt. Eliza, they could hardly fail to have been exhilarated by such a superb waterway.

Not only was the Swan quite breathtakingly beautiful, but it promised picnics by the waterside, fishing at dusk, gay river cruises, refreshing bathing, thrilling regattas and, most importantly, an easily navigable 'highway' in a colony without roads.

*Seals bask undisturbed on an island close to Perth.*

Captain James Stirling was one of the first to establish his family home on its banks. He nostalgically named it Woodbridge after his wife's family home in Surrey. In 1885 Stirling's "cottage ornée" was replaced by an imposing late Victorian-style family home which still graces a scenic bend of the river at Guildford.

## THE MAGIC OF "THE SWAN"

All those early expectations of the Swan River have been generously fulfilled. In every sense, it has become the focal point of Perth life... the source of hours of leisure enjoyment for all ages, and a sparkling backdrop for the city's commercial heart and thousands of homes spread along its reaches.

Everyone can find a favourite spot for more than 80% of the river front is public property.

On any sunny Saturday afternoon, the true value of the river to Perth reveals itself, for that's the time when all ages gravitate to enjoy its magic. Family groups settle down under the shady peppermint trees of Mosman Bay to paddle, swim and gaze at yachtsmen busying themselves around their boats in the nearby yacht club.

Out in Melville Water and Matilda Bay yachts of all sizes billow vivid-hued spinnakers as they scud before the wind. Catamarans, tiny sailing dinghies and glamorous, streamlined ocean-goers maneouvre to catch the shifting wind in a game which holds its fascination week after week, year after year.

The weekend mass of colourful sails against the backdrop of the city skyline is one of Perth's most spectacular moods.

The river isn't only for sail. Power boats race up and down selected river stretches in the quest for exhilarating speed. Many tow skiers and others launch hang gliders to soar high above the shimmering water before gliding down to a gentle landing.

As dusk descends, the skiers, yachtsmen, swimmers and boaters give way to the fishermen and parties laden with lamps and nets as the Swan takes on another, more restful guise. It's the hour for prawning, crabbing and reeling in kingfish, tailer and bream, for the river is rich in marine life. Children dangling handlines over the edge of a jetty are just as hopeful of 'landing a big one' as their fathers casting professionally from the shore.

The absence of industry along any length of the river explains the Swan's clear, untainted water after 150 years of settlement. Perth's heavy industry is all centred at Kwinana, 40 kms south of the city, far from its precious waterway. Where other cities pollute their rivers with oil-oozing cargo boats, the port of Fremantle, 19 kms from the capital's centre handles all shipping. Sleek passenger liners and container vessels berth in the inner harbour just around the corner from sturdy fishing boats anchored in Fishermen's Harbour.

Such planning foresight has made Perth's clean air and fish-filled waterways the envy of many cities. The only major commercial craft entitled to use the river are ferries, plying upriver into the Swan Valley, across from the business district to the southern shoreline and downriver to the Indian Ocean.

## VINES BY THE RIVERSIDE

A leisurely ferry trip upriver to the fertile Swan Valley reveals a quieter, more elusive aspect of the Swan.

This is Perth's vineyard country, the home of widely-fancied Houghton, Valencia and Sandalford vintages and many others popular with West Australian wine drinkers.

Some of the picturesque wineries nestling in the foothills of the Darling Range are among the oldest in Australia. Vines were first planted at Olive Farm on the banks of the Swan in 1829 and the first vintage was ready for sampling in 1833. The winery still produces a regular range of award-winning styles.

Each autumn, the Swan Valley hosts a rollicking weekend wine festival. Wine lovers boat upriver to join in the eating, drinking, dancing and grape stomping which continue long into the night. To many of the vignerons, migrants from Italy and Yugoslavia, the festival relives memories of christening the new wine at home.

Evening river cruises have been a Swan tradition since the early colonists steamed decorously downriver in such craft as 'The Decoy' and 'The Enchantress.' Nowadays, the wine flows more freely and the music pounds out with more zest, but the old romance of moonlight and rippling water is just as beguiling as ever.

## PERTH'S "ENCHANTED" ISLAND

Several large ferries ply the regular "Rottnest run," the 18 km ocean crossing to Western Australia's delightful holiday island. In the height of summer, they are packed each day with holidaymakers off to enjoy its simple pleasures of swimming, fishing, bicycling and camping out under the stars.

Rottnest has not always been the holiday paradise it is today. During the colony's early days, "Rotto" served as a gaol for Aboriginal prisoners and many old buildings were built by their forced labour.

Beach towels and bikinis now hang out to dry in The Quad, a quaint octagonal building which once served as the island prison. The guest rooms are the original cells where prisoners were shackled each night in crowded, stifling conditions.

Away from the old prison, the island reveals an unexpected touch of colonial splendour! It was decided the colony's Governor needed a cool summer retreat to forget the burdens of duty, so a vice-regal summer Residence was constructed for that purpose in 1864. Today, this grand old building is the island hotel, the universally loved "Quokka Arms." Its strange name derives from the small rock wallaby, or quokka, which abounds on Rottnest to the delight of visitors.

## AN OCEAN ON THE DOORSTEP

The regular weekend pilgrimage to Rottnest reveals Perth's strong affinity with the Indian Ocean which surges against a coastline more than 6,000 kilometres long. The combination of sun, surf and shimmering white sand exerts a magnetic pull for thousands during the summer months.

Sun seekers have an enviable choice of where to spend their day, as Perth's suburban beaches stretch along 50 kms of easily accessible coastline from Coogee in the south to Mullaloo in the north. And all the way it's a sparkling playground of green surf, white sand and vivid blue sky.

When the temperature soars, people flock to the ocean for the tantalising coolness of a quick dip. Yet, even on the hottest day, there's sure to be a stretch of sand secluded from the crowds, a rocky cove all to yourself.

Each beach has its own particular character to attract a band of devotees. The surfers of Scarborough or Triggs would never desert their rolling ocean breakers for the calmer shallows of Cottesloe. And nor is it likely to be the other way round.

The early-morning, all-year-round swimmers are a different breed. A hardiness bred from plunging into the surf on even the bitterest winter mornings, unites them in a common bond. Businessmen, housewives and retired workers meet each morning for their ritual swim and jog, long before the city stirs.

With Western Australia's vast stretch of coastline, it's no surprise to see seafood on almost every restaurant menu. Schnapper, skipjack, tailer, herring, whiting and probably the favourite of them all, succulent jewfish, bring success to almost every fishing trip. Anglers cast from suburban beaches or groynes jutting metres out into the sea as dawn begins to brighten the horizon.

Other seafood lovers fancy shellfish and Indian Ocean waters are rich with rock lobster, prawns, mussels and tasty blue manna crabs. A feast of fresh-cooked prawns washed down with ice-cold beer is a real Western Australian speciality.

*The thrill of a fair wind on the ocean waters of Cockburn Sound.*

And, of course, yachtsmen have their own special preserve on the ocean. At Cockburn Sound, just south of Fremantle, experienced blue water sailors and "weekenders" jostle for the most favoured starting position as the weekend racing gets under way. The Sound has hosted national yachting championships and is the setting for the State's largest regatta held annually during the Christmas holiday break.

Travel posters showing glossy tanned bodies cavorting on the water, paint a true picture of Perth in the summer. What they miss, however, are the city's winter moods. A bracing westerly howling in off the ocean or the spectacle of the Swan whipped up into "whitecaps" are just as close to the heart of Perth. To the people who live in this lucky city, their water setting is a year-long love affair.

On pages 68 and 69 following: City office towers gaze down on this scene of early morning tranquillity on the Swan.

The relentless ocean has carved this striking sandstone formation at Safety Bay.

Left: The broad Swan River harbours many yacht clubs. At Claremont, yachts swing at anchor against a backdrop of reflected light.

Just up the river at Royal Perth Yacht Club, crews prepare for another exhilarating day.

Life centres on the river at luxurious
Mosman Park.

"Gone crabbing." A feast of crabs or prawns
is a summer evening speciality.

Left: Indian Ocean surf is a pleasure
thousands enjoy every weekend.

Relaxation is an art at Rottnest Island,
Perth's offshore holiday playground.

Right: Long before the city stirs, water birds are breakfasting by the edge of the river.

On page 78 following: The river offers a rich harvest of shellfish on any summer evening.

On page 80 following: Picnickers can lunch in peaceful bushland, a morning's drive from Perth.

The many bays of the Swan provide safe mooring for thousands of pleasure craft.

# DAYDREAMS AND NIGHTLIFE

A first-time visitor to Perth could be forgiven for believing its people spent all their waking hours enjoying "the great outdoors."

After all, there's so much of it to enjoy and such a wonderful climate in which to appreciate it.

As every travel brochure highlights, Perth is Australia's sunniest capital, basking in a daily average of eight hours' sunshine. Even the winters are Mediterranean-mild with rain pouring itself out in a few days of heavy downpours. Most winter days are crisp and sunny, inviting a leisurely stroll through city parks or an energetic afternoon of sport.

Indeed, one early government official was moved to describe the climate in a most un-public service lyrical vein. Mr. W. E. Cook, the Government Astronomer wrote in 1901—"In the Southern and especially southwestern portions of the State we find a climate which for agricultural, horticultural or ordinary living purposes is probably unsurpassed in the world."

Most people in Perth today would agree with him and fashion their lifestyles to enjoy sunshine to the full.

## LEISURELY LIVING

Picnics, bushwalking, barbecues, outdoor festivals, pool parties and of course sport, on land and water, dominate leisure moments.

The scenic Darling Range is honeycombed with delightful picnic spots all within a short drive of the city. Walking tracks wind through dense native growth which in spring blazes in a mass of gold, white, crimson and even sky-blue wildflowers.

Other picnickers prefer to "make a day of it" at Yanchep, north of Perth. Wide shaded lawns, a congenial pub, underground caverns and a wildlife sanctuary "starring" cuddly koala bears offer a diversion for every taste. A large lake with row boats for hire is the beautiful centrepiece of Yanchep and a highlight of the day's outing.

A few kilometres further on, yachts bob at their moorings in a marina built on a superb ocean beach setting. Western Australia's 1977 America's Cup challenger, Australia, sailed thousands of trial hours in these waters in preparation for her gallant but unsuccessful battle at Newport, Rhode Island.

The yachting enthusiasm of recent years is only one aspect of Perth's long sport-loving tradition. Since the first horse race meeting was organised in 1833, sport has mushroomed in popularity and variety.

Hockey and soccer fields, tennis and squash courts, bowling greens, cricket and football ovals and golf courses are dotted throughout the suburbs to cater to a multitude of participants.

Cricket, one of the colony's earliest pastimes, has blossomed into a sporting success story for Western Australia.

The State team has regular success in the fiercely-contested interstate Sheffield Shield competition, and in recent years, has consistently provided the backbone of Australian Test sides. Dennis Lillee and Rod Marsh, once mercurial stars of the Test arena, are top-line drawcards in World Series Cricket, based in Perth at Gloucester Park.

Gloucester Park is also Australia's premier pacing track. Family groups and the keenest punters take up vantage points on the lawns to savour the thrill of horses and "spiders" pacing furiously around the brilliantly-lit track. Others sit in comfort over a glass of wine and a three-course meal as the race unfolds itself on colour television screens in the comfortably-appointed upstairs restaurant. At Gloucester Park it is hardly necessary to even bet to enjoy a night out at "the Trots."

Football fever takes hold in the winter months as eight teams battle for the Australian Rules premiership. On Grand Final day, thousands stream into Subiaco Oval to shout themselves hoarse urging their teams on to superhuman efforts. When it's all over, the streamers left testify to a great day's fun for all.

*A flight of fancy during Perth's colourful Christmas Pageant.*

## ARTISTIC UNDERCURRENTS

The sporting enthusiasm which grips most of its citizens is the brasher, noisier aspect of Perth.

Beneath the bravado lies the city's subtler side, the world of lunch-time recitals, of quiet suburban art galleries, of outdoor craft festivals where potters turn their wheels, silversmiths fashion delicate jewellery and leatherworkers tool belts and bags.

The three-day Hyde Park Festival is one of many such events which give free-and-easy expression to the city's vibrant cultural life. Local artisans set up stalls under shady Moreton Bay Fig trees as ethnic dance groups entertain the crowd with vivid costumes and spirited dance.

Perth's artistic vitality stems partly from top-class venues, but more importantly, from a blossoming community interest in the Arts.

The growth of interest began with the opening of the Perth Concert Hall, a venue of international standard for solo performers, jazz combos, symphony concerts and spectacular folk dance companies.

Entertainment on a grander scale takes place under the vast canopy of the 8,000 capacity Perth Entertainment Centre. Rock concerts, ballets, tennis, gymnastics and a galaxy of the world's greatest circus performers have drawn capacity audiences to fill the huge auditorium.

An annual highlight, the Prom concerts, illustrates the versatility of the Centre as hundreds bring cushions and bean bags to settle in comfort on the floor and enjoy popular classics in the informal atmosphere.

The charming studios and sheltered courtyards of the Fremantle Arts Centre provide artistic stimulus for weavers, leatherworkers, painters, spinners, potters and creative writers. The Centre has been imaginatively restored to rank as one of Australia's finest colonial-gothic buildings.

*Andalusian dancing horses at El Caballo Blanco, a Spanish-style hotel in hills near Perth.*

## A CARNIVAL OF THE ARTS

Each summer, Perth's cultural energy crystallizes in the Festival of Perth. Overseas and local artists draw enthusiastic audiences to many of the city's finest venues...the thrust stage Octagon Theatre where Shakespeare seems to have found his ideal milieu, the Playhouse, home of the State's National Theatre, and the New Fortune Theatre, a replica within the University of Western Australia of the original Fortune theatre of Shakespeare's London. Theatre groups find its jutting stage and overhead balconies an exhilarating setting for imaginative drama.

During the university term the New Fortune is surrounded by study rooms. Occasionally, the studious quiet is shattered by the harsh, barking cry of a peacock, once used as an authentic prop in an Elizabethan production. The peacock and his mate have grown so attached to their new "home," they have adopted it as their nesting ground.

Balmy summer evenings draw thousands of Festival patrons to lie back on the lawns of Supreme Court Gardens as brass bands and full orchestras perform in an open-air orchestral shell. Cinema fans congregate at the Somerville Auditorium where the heady scent of pine from surrounding trees adds further charm to the evening's viewing.

Concerts, jazz, ballet, opera and art and craft exhibitions all attract keen support during the Festival months.

The beautiful garden setting of the University of Western Australia is a year-long venue for artistic expression. The grounds contain three theatres, including the highly innovative Octagon, a delightful amphitheatre and countless courtyards which lend themselves to many uses.

Perth has recently re-opened another theatre to boost its already-imposing list of theatrical venues. His Majesty's Theatre, beloved by ballet and musical comedy fans for most of the century, is being remodelled by the State Government at a cost of almost $5 million. The "Maj's" ornate interior will be revamped while preserving the distinctive atmosphere of Australia's only surviving Edwardian theatre.

## BARS, BISTROS...AND BACH

The theatre crowds merge with winers, diners and dancers as Perth's pace quickens into its evening moods. Exuberant dancers whirl away the hours in fashionable nightclubs while others prefer the soothing melodies of a late-night piano bar. International-standard hotels offer a selection of fine restaurants and stylish dance spots where overseas travellers rub shoulders with local revellers. Many younger people enjoy the conviviality of taverns and wine bars where singing along with the band is a prime attraction.

Music for every taste finds expression in Perth. The Concert Hall and the University of Western Australia's Winthrop Hall are regular venues for concerts and recitals. Jazz fans cram happily into tiny, smoke-filled clubs where their music seems so much more at home than the echoing spaces of a concert platform.

Dining out, too, is a memorable pleasure in Perth. It's often said that Perth has more restaurants per head than any other Australian city. And the variety of food available seems to bear out this boast. Italian, French, Chinese, Yugoslav, Mexican, Spanish, Greek, Lebanese, Hungarian, Japanese, even Polynesian...every great cuisine and some of lesser reputation have found their way to Perth.

A short walk north of the city centre and you'll find yourself in the heart of Perth's restaurant district. Sometimes six or seven restaurants in a single street try to outdo each other with tempting menus of Western Australian seafoods, provincial French dishes or perhaps an exotic Balkan speciality.

And, as a finishing touch, you can stroll out for a Lebanese pastry or a mouth-tingling gelati, freshly made in a nearby cafe.

Many restaurants follow the bistro tradition of "Bring your own" to keep the cost of dining out within the reach of almost every family. Yet, for a special occasion, a variety of elegant eating spots serve gourmet dishes accompanied by the finest French and Australian wines. Local wines appear more frequently than in the past on restaurant wine lists. Together with its heritage of Swan Valley wines, Western Australia now has a new wine-growing area in the cooler South-West region. Outstanding wines from such areas as Frankland River and Mount Barker are achieving increasing acclaim throughout Australia.

Perth people are aware of all their city offers. More than most city dwellers they have the joy of sun-filled days...and a seemingly endless variety of evening fun with no fears as darkness falls.

Weekend sport in the centre of the city
on the wide playing fields of Langley Park.

On pages 84 and 85 following: A simple
celebration of Christmas...Carols by Candlelight in the city's Supreme Court Gardens.

Surfing catamarans are popular at Yanchep,
the base for Alan Bond's America's Cup
challenge in 1977.

Enthusiastic supporters enjoy the spectacle
of "Aussie Rules" football.

Left: Relaxed informality at one of Perth's regular outdoor craft festivals.

Trotting is high-excitement action at Gloucester Park, also the Perth home of World Series Cricket.

Concentrating on pottery during a
school craft class.

The annual Festival of Perth caters to every
musical taste. Here, bandsmen perform in
Supreme Court Gardens.

Right: Floodlit artistry on the stage of the
University of Western Australia's Sunken
Garden Theatre.

On page 94 following: Enjoying the view from
Kings Park over the City of Perth and its
sparkling waterways.

After dark glamour in one of Perth's many
elegant nightspots.

# A PARK FOR ALL SEASONS

A love of greenery and wide open spaces has been ingrained in Perth from the earliest days.

In 1899, a huge area of native bushland on the heights of Mount Eliza overlooking the Swan River, was set aside as a public park. Kings Park stands today as a superb monument to the foresight of the city's founders.

Covering more than 400 hectares, the park is one of the glories of Perth. Every age group can find some area of particular interest... a view, a playground, or perhaps the tinkling fascination of a fountain.

Walking tracks wind through untouched native bushland which, each spring, blossoms into a profusion of colour with Western Australia's world-famous wildflowers. Banksias, bottlebrushes, wattles, orchids, myrtles, leschenaultia and the striking dark red and green Kangaroo Paw, W.A.'s floral emblem, attract bushwalkers and nature lovers from all over the world to marvel at their beauty.

*Soaring high above the city against a backdrop of Mt. Eliza.*

Kings Park contains many of the 7,000 species of flowering trees and plants which are found only in Western Australia. They have evolved over countless ages in total isolation from the rest of the world.

Native trees and plants and many imported species are displayed in more formal arrangements in the delightful Botanic Gardens which sweep gently down the face of Mount Eliza. The Pioneer Women's Fountain, one of Perth's most dramatic outdoor sculptures, blends harmoniously into the landscaped surroundings of lakes and undulating lawns and gardens. By night, it provides a spectacular play of coloured lights.

Children, too, have their own special area in the park. An imaginative playground tempts the adventurous with its bold arrangements of natural wood. Those with plenty of energy can climb an unusual lookout which spirals high into the sky in the shape of the DNA molecule.

Kings Park's setting high above Perth affords spectacular views over the city and the Swan River. Each year more than five million people visit the park making it one of the most-used urban parks in Australia. Many come just to enjoy the superb panorama over the office towers and curving freeways of the city skyline. The shimmering, deep-blue water of the Swan River seen from the crest of Kings Park is just as beautiful to local people as to visitors viewing the scene for the very first time.

At night, the city transforms itself into a mass of twinkling, coloured lights, a postcard scene which has made Perth famous throughout the world. Diners in the park's own restaurant can relish the spectacle while enjoying a leisurely meal.

Kings Park's central location only a brisk walk from the commercial heart of St. George's Terrace, together with its many facilities for weekend enjoyment make it a vital hub of Perth life. The decision to preserve the natural bush for eternity as a public park has added an immeasurable delight to the city's life.

## A GARDEN UNIVERSITY

Just minutes away along the river foreshore lies Perth's first university, the University of Western Australia.

The campus is regarded as probably the most beautiful in Australia, and many students come back year after year just to enjoy its relaxing atmosphere. Attractive limestone buildings in the older section of the campus are uniformly Mediterranean in design and fringed by lush green lawns and large formal garden beds. The Great Court in the centre of the university grounds is a stimulating setting for outdoor seminars and even the occasional heated student political meeting. New faculty buildings incorporate courtyards and fountains to harmonise with the picturesque surroundings.

Hidden away from the bustle is one of the university's most delightful attractions, the Sunken Garden theatre, a favourite outdoor venue for ballet, theatre, and boisterous folk music. On a warm summer evening with a cool breeze just stirring the leaves of the overhanging trees, the garden attains an almost magical charm. A performance of Macbeth achieves the chilling eeriness Shakespeare intended when "witches" wail from high up in the branches of a shadowy tree.

## RELAXING IN THE CITY

Perth is one of those rare places where relaxation in the city centre can be a rich experience.

One of the earliest of Perth's parks, the Stirling Gardens is handy to the business district at the corner of St. George's Terrace and Barrack Street.

Each lunch hour the benches, garden chairs and rolling green lawns are crowded with workers

Just a short walk from the city is one
of the many relaxing places in beautiful
Kings Park.

enjoying a respite from their airconditioned offices.

The Gardens were founded in 1845 and many early pioneers took a keen interest in planting different species of trees and plants. The first Surveyor-General, John Septimus Roe, a keen horticulturist, personally planted many of the largest trees. He exchanged seeds of native trees for those of European species and thereby established a trend for exotic trees in many of Perth's parks. The Gardens once served a botanical function where such plants as olives and vines were grown to test their suitability to Western Australian soils. Today, however, these Gardens and the adjoining Supreme Court Gardens are intended solely for enjoyment. And, for many, that means lolling back on the soft grass and engaging in the age-old pastime of 'bird-watching.'

Just before Christmas, flickering candlelight bathes the sprawling lawns in a soft, mellow glow. "Carols by Candlelight" is an annual joy for families who come in their thousands to join in the spirit of the festive season.

The influence of the first English colonists is particularly evident in another city park, Queens Gardens.

Situated at the eastern end of the city centre, the park gives the impression of being a "little piece of England" transported to a far-flung colony. Oak and plane trees are laid out in the style of a formal garden among tranquil lakes bedecked with water lilies. Small bridges link the islands and a replica of the Peter Pan statue of London's Kensington Gardens adds a distinctive charm. The Gardens are a favourite setting for wedding photographs and Saturday afternoon strollers can share for a few moments the beaming happiness of a bridal party.

Big shady European trees make Hyde Park, in the inner city suburb of Highgate, a haven from the summer heat.

A large lake and unusual wading pools for children attract many family groups for weekend picnics. Hyde Park is especially popular with Italian, Greek and Yugoslav communities who live in the neighbouring suburbs of North Perth, Mt Lawley and Highgate. During one holiday weekend each March, the park temporarily loses its tranquil peace and hosts a festival of arts, crafts, music, dance and general merrymaking. Perth's migrant groups provide much of the entertainment for this Hyde Park Festival.

## WILDLIFE IN A GARDEN SETTING

Black swans, the instantly identifiable symbol of Western Australia, are an appealing attraction at Lake Monger, a few kilometres west of the city. The large lake is a haven for birdlife, providing a safe refuge only a brief walk from busy traffic. Many of the swans and wild ducks are tame enough to feed by hand.

A glimpse of a long-necked tortoise waddling purposefully through the long reeds can be a rare pleasure. The natural bushland of Perth's largest park, Bold Park, bordering the suburbs of Floreat and City Beach, provides delightful walks among native birds and animals.

Exotic wildlife is on permanent view at Perth's Zoological Gardens, across the river from the city at South Perth. A nocturnal animal house gives the wildlife lover a rare opportunity to glimpse the usually "invisible" creatures of the animal kingdom. Of course, no zoo would be complete without its lovable elephants, giraffes, monkeys, zebras and fearsome wild cats. At the Perth Zoo these creatures and many others are housed among tall trees and rolling green lawns in a garden setting. Part of the joy of a day's outing to the zoo is the 15 minute ferry trip across the river, incomparable on a crisp spring morning.

## NATURE UNTOUCHED

Apart from formal parks and gardens, Perth people have a wide choice of nearby national parks and nature reserves for a pleasant afternoon's ramble. John Forrest National Park, named after a noted explorer who became the State's first Premier, covers a wide area of bushland in the Darling Range. Streams, waterfalls and a natural swimming pool make it a delightful weekend picnic spot.

Canoeists are attracted by the swirling rapids of Walyunga National Park which sits astride the fast-flowing Avon River. Heavy winter rains turn the water into a foaming torrent which provides a challenging course for the annual 95 kilometre Avon Descent.

The picturesque water catchment of Serpentine Dam and the pine tree beauty of Mundaring Weir are popular with picnickers. Mundaring is the source of the water pipeline to the arid Goldfields, 550

*The dominating presence of Lord Forrest, famous explorer and first Premier of Western Australia.*

kilometres from Perth. During the gold rushes of the 1890's, when rich finds lured thousands of fortune hunters, water came to be more precious than gold itself in the overcrowded camps. The pipeline was built in 1902 and has ever since been the lifeline'for such towns as Kalgoorlie and Boulder.

The vision and achievements of Perth's early generations have created a city where the living really is easy...where twentieth century progress and age-old natural beauty blend in a delicate harmony.

Left: Winthrop Hall sets a Mediterranean tone on the beautiful garden campus of the University of Western Australia.

On pages 100 and 101 following:
Evening shadows lengthen in one of Perth's many suburban parks.

Perth City Council's 27 hole golf course and driving range at Wembley is one of the finest in the country.

Left: The Harold Boas Gardens are a refreshing stroll from the commercial centre of West Perth.

Native waterfowl are unperturbed by freeways ringing their man-made lake in the heart of the city.

The small ones don't get away at
Perry Lakes, a rambling area of parkland
and playing fields close to the city.

The rugged Avon Descent, which finishes
on Perth Water, is an annual test of
endurance for canoeists and power boat drivers.

A barbecue lunch under a canopy of stately
gums in Kings Park.

Right: After winter rains in the Darling Ranges.

On page 110 following: The Pioneer Women's Fountain, Kings Park, a spectacular tribute to the founding women of Western Australia.

Peter Pan, a replica of the London original, holds an enduring fascination in Queens Gardens.

# PERTH UNLIMITED

One hundred and fifty years have passed and Perth is only just stepping out on the road to greatness.

As the capital of a vast State blessed with immense mineral wealth, Perth's future stretches towards a limitless horizon.

Raw materials from the Pilbara region in the north of the State alone guarantee prosperity till at least the 21st century. Iron ore created the "industrial revolution" of the past decade, but now it is only part of the mineral spectrum paving the way to industrial might.

In the next decade it is predicted that between $4,000 million and $8,000 million will be invested in new mining ventures and the industries that will develop from them. The impact of these enormous sums injected into the State's economy will generate a burgeoning new phase in the history of Perth.

Yet the sort of uncontrolled growth which has ruined so many cities as a living environment seems an impossible prospect for Perth. The Perth public has shown itself in recent years to be increasingly aware of the beauty of the city... and the need to preserve it. Vocal community groups have protested against the encroachment of major roads onto private property and scenic riverside land. Others have taken up the cause of the Swan River and, with the help of the Swan River Management Authority zealously guard their superb waterway from pollution and erosion. The State Government has formed a Department of Environmental Protection to guard against the demands of industry. Unlittered street verges and meticulously kept front gardens show a keen respect for an environment where all can enjoy the striking visual beauty of Perth.

Ironically, it took the mineral bonanza of the 1960's to spark Perth's environmental concern. Rapid industrial and residential growth made people aware of the charm they stood to lose if development raged unchecked.

Their concern spread outwards from the city to encompass bushland, beaches, rivers and lakes throughout the State. Now, Western Australia has a greater proportion of land safeguarded as national parks or nature reserves than any other State. Unique animal and birdlife and extraordinary natural phenomena such as the petrified tree trunks of the Pinnacles Desert in Nambung National Park are preserved for generations to come.

The "Roaring Sixties" had another, just as lasting, effect on Perth. Mineral finds brought an influx of migrants eager to earn big money toiling in the baking heat and clinging red dust of the North. Most of those who came from Italy, Greece and Yugoslavia were vigorous young men and women who stayed to raise families and fashion a new life in their land of promise. Their contribution has been far-reaching.

Together with older generations who sought refuge in Perth from war-torn Europe, the new migrants have shaped the city into a vibrant cosmopolitan society. Restaurants, the Arts, festivals, fashion, entertaining at home and an increasing capacity for hard work all reflect the influence of a multi-racial culture.

Perth's pre-war Anglo-Saxon conservatism which permeated every aspect of life has largely disappeared under the impact of new ideas. The traditional 1950's restaurant fare of prawns and steak has given way to an enticing array of French bouillabaisse, Greek moussaka, Indian curries and Dutch-Indonesian rijstafel. New restaurants open almost weekly in Perth as an indication of the popularity of eating out.

Outmoded licensing laws have given way to an enlightened approach in recent years. Hotels stay open till midnight and later, and taverns, nightclubs and wine bars offer fun-seekers a wide choice of food, drink and entertainment.

Entertaining at home has been revolutionised. Cooking courses, especially Chinese and provincial French, are immensely popular with housewives and young couples eager to entertain family and friends. Woks, terrine dishes and souffle bowls take pride of place in many kitchens relegating faithful old saucepans and frying pans to a dark shelf.

The European influence has extended into the Arts, where concerts, exhibitions, exciting theatre and innovative dance express a vibrant creative force. Such festivals as the German community's "Oktoberfest" and the Swan Valley "Vintage" annually enliven Perth's spirit with the flavour and fun of European tradition.

*The sparkle of Christmas in Hay Street Mall.*

The merging of many cultures has had a subtler impact, one that has passed unnoticed by many Perth people. Sharing a school desk or living next door to a Giovanni or a Hans has broadened the outlook of many of Anglo-Saxon heritage and created a city where tolerance is a byword. Polish, Spanish and Yugoslav school friends and workmates are never thought of as migrants, but simply as "New Australians" sharing the riches of a bountiful land.

Since the Sixties, Western Australia's ties have stretched out to encompass Asia, especially Japan. As the State's biggest market for her raw materials, Japan has assumed vital importance to Western Australia.

Moonlit serenity over the City of Lights.

Overseas visitors and locals enjoy world-class hotel facilities.

The economic ties have grown with time and trust into cultural and artistic bonds. Japanese rooms and traditional rock gardens have been incorporated into the University of Western Australia and the Western Australian Institute of Technology to encourage the study of Japanese culture. The serenity of the surroundings is an inspiration to students tackling the difficulties of Japanese language.

Perth's ties to Japan have been cemented in a "Sister City" link with Kagoshima, the southernmost city of Kyushu Island.

The liaison, first suggested by a Kagoshima trade mission to Perth, was formalised in an agreement signed by the Lord Mayor of Perth and the Mayor of Kagoshima in 1974. The aim is pure idealism, a rare commodity in most international links. In the words of the agreement, the Sister City pact is aimed at "promoting an example of international goodwill which will help in achieving a lasting peace among the nations of Asia." Reciprocal visits by individuals and groups and exchanges of tape recordings and letters among school children over thousands of miles of ocean, have strengthened this unique bond, and helped make Japanese thought and culture an exciting educational challenge for an increasing number of West Australians.

South East Asian conflicts have brought Vietnamese and Timorese refugees to Perth. After initial language difficulties and "culture shock," the refugees have settled easily into the melting pot of Perth society.

The greater diversity of taste and opinion which is the result of all these influences, is very apparent in Western Australia's education system. Perth's second university, Murdoch, has moved away from the traditional academic role to direct itself to the wider community. Its courses are highly flexible and designed to appeal equally to young students straight out of school and housewives and retired workers keen to resume an interrupted education.

The traditional academic role is pursued by the University of Western Australia, while practical professional training is the forte of the Western Australian Institute of Technology.

Perth's "coming of age" as an international city dates from the 1960's when mineral finds lured overseas interest and investment. This decade of dramatic growth saw five-star international hotels spring up to cater for businessmen, trade delegations and full-scale conventions.

When the hardy pioneers built their crude shelters on the banks of the Swan 150 years ago, they were building the most isolated city in the world. Thousands of miles of turbulent ocean separated the fledgling colony from the nearest land, and a vast desert stretched toward the eastern horizon. The isolation bred a fighting spirit, a dogged determination to build a city despite the odds.

Today, the City of Perth is a superb monument to their strength of will. In just 150 years, it has grown from isolation to take its place in the whirl of international commerce, trade and tourism. The next 150 years hold the promise of even more dramatic change as Perth reaches out ever further into the tide of international affairs.

Right: Gardens soften the cut glass lines
of striking city architecture.

On pages 116 and 117 following:
Silhouettes of industry mellowed by an
evening glow at Kwinana.

The North West Shelf natural gas field is the
scene of Australia's greatest natural
resource project.

Left: Mining on a massive scale in the iron-ore mountains of the Pilbara.

Dawn breaks over smoking furnaces at the Kwinana industrial complex, just south of Perth.

Western Australia's Parliament House
commands a sweeping view over Perth city
and the Swan River.

Comfort and colour welcome interstate train
passengers at the modern Westrail terminal
at East Perth.

On page 124 following:
Dawn over Perth heralds a new era of
excitement.

Lights merge in ribbons of colour as traffic
sweeps across modern freeways linking city
and suburbs.